Predator-Proofing

A HANDBOOK

Diane Roblin-Lee
Foreword by
Melodie Bissell

Predator-Proof Your Family Series
#3 Predator-Proofing our Children
Copyright ©2018 Diane Roblin-Lee

ISBN 978-1-896213-50-7   E-book ISBN 978-1-896213-62-0

PUBLISHED IN CANADA
byDesign Media
www.bydesignmedia.ca
First Edition 2009
Second Edition 2018

COVER DESIGN — Diane Roblin-Lee

Cataloguing data available from Library and Archives Canada

Purpose

The eightfold purpose behind the
Predator-Proof Your Family Series:

- To help families and guardians recognize danger signs in people who have access to the children in their care

- To deter people who are fantasizing about molesting a child from acting on their fantasies

- To protect children from molestation through raising awareness on many levels

- To be aware of the new challenges of parenting in the 21st-century.

- To deepen the understanding of all levels of society affected by the molestation of a child

- To find healing for victims and families

- To encourage the kind of justice and community action that prevents potential or convicted predators from initial offending and re-offending.

- To demonstrate to all those who have been molested that we care deeply about what you have endured and, in honour of you, are doing all we can to protect other children from sharing your experience.

Predator-Proof Your Family Booklet Series

by Diane Roblin-Lee

Booklet #1 – *Why All the Fuss?* ISBN 978-1-896213-48-4
Prevalence, Effects and Trends of Child Sexual Abuse

Booklet #2 – *Who is the Predator?* ISBN 978-1-896213-49-1
Identification – Warning Signs

Booklet #3 – *Predator-Proofing Our Children* ISBN 978-1-896213-50-7
Recognizing the Grooming Process
Parent / Child Education – When the Molester Strikes at Home

Booklet #4 – *Predators in Pews and Pulpits* ISBN 978-1-896213-51-4
The God Factor - Forgiveness?
How Dare They Call Themselves Christians?

Booklet #5 – *The Porn Factor* ISBN 978-1-896213-52-1
Are You Raising a Predator?
The Old Bottom Line - The Buck

Booklet #6 – *It's All About the Brain* ISBN 978-1-896213-53-8
Does Child Molestation Affect Brain Development?
How to Use the Brain in Effective Treatment

Booklet #7 – *When the Worst That Can Happen Has Already Happened*
ISBN 978-1-896213-54-5   Healing for the Victim
Parenting an Abused Child – Coping as the Family of a Predator

Booklet #8 – *Smart Justice* ISBN 978-1-896213-47-7
Community Response to Predators Who Have Served Their Time
Church Response - School Response - Restorative Justice

Booklet #9 – *The Husband I Never Knew* ISBN 978-1-896213-56-9
The true story of Diane Roblin-Lee, ex-wife of a man who, after 38
years of marriage, confessed to being a child molester.

Available online in Paperback, Kindle and E-Pub
Also available through Plan to Protect®
177 Ringwood Dr., Unit #11, Stouffville, ON CAN L4A 8C1
www.plantoprotect.com 1-877-455-3555

Foreword

Bubble gum pizza!!

Have you ever even considered ordering one? For fifteen years my children knew this was the secret phrase that anyone who might say they were given directions by Mom and Dad to pick them up, would have to know.

We talked about "bubble gum pizza" often in our home. The secret code was known only amongst the five of us. We were committed to sharing the phrase only if we were to need to ask another adult to pick up our children. The children knew they must ask for the secret code before going with anyone. If the person knew the code, the children knew they were safe to travel with them.

Now that they are adults, we no longer need our children to remember the code. As I write this, I whisper a prayer of thanks that we never needed to use it.

With *Predator-Proofing our Children*, Diane Roblin-Lee has done it again. She has provided an excellent resource to equip parents with tips for predator-proofing their children. Providing a secret code is not enough. Having a full understanding of the issues involved is essential to ensure our children's safety.

How much preparedness is too much? As a mom, I never wanted regrets. I always did my utmost to protect my children. Early on, my mother-in-law shared her story with me and her experience drove me to greater vigilance than I might otherwise have exerted. She shared with me about the abuse she endured in the 1930's at the hands of a boarder in their home. She said, "I didn't have the vocabulary to tell anyone. We never talked about sex. My parents would have thought it was incomprehensible that someone would take advantage of me under their own roof. When the abuse began, I tried to tell my teacher and brothers, as well as the parents of my close friends. No one would believe me. I then told my pastor's wife and she believed me. She didn't ask if I was lying! Oh how I loved that dear woman."

How many children carry secrets of abuse? How many of our children are we handing over to predators naively? How many other children do not have the vocabulary to tell of the abuse?

It is a wise mom and dad who take the God-given responsibility to protect their children seriously.

I urge parents to guard against any possibility of incurring regrets. It's so important to carefully screen anyone allowed into a child's world; whether a relative, a person of faith, or a 'good Samaritan.' Children have been entrusted into our care.

My hope with the *Predator-Proof Your Family* series is that parents and care-givers will invest added time and energy into learning how to protect their children. If only one child is spared from abuse, the series will be well worth all the time, effort and research.

On behalf of the children,
Melodie Bissell

President, *Plan to Protect*®
www.plantoprotect.com

Predator-Proofing our Children

Incredibly, we entrust the identification of pedophiles to the smallest, most vulnerable members of society – our children. We think that by teaching them about "good touch/bad touch," how to say "no," and to tell us if anyone crosses the line, we can train them to be responsible for their own protection. Then we relax, thinking our kids have been empowered and know how to keep safe – and that we've done our jobs.

But we have lulled ourselves to sleep. It's not enough. I did all that with my children and grandchildren – and still, two of them were victimized over long periods of time, not knowing how to tell.

For a child, having been told what to do when someone crosses the line does not translate into taking steps to protect or defend themselves, or to telling someone what has happened. The situations in which children can be trapped by intimidating, manipulative child abusers can be too complex for honest responses. The emotions stirred by a predator can be horribly confusing for innocent children, to the extent that they have no idea what to do, even though they may have been told precisely what to do.

There is no proof that "bad touch" warnings prevent child sexual abuse. Available data shows that few children are able to learn to apply this training before the third grade. I was unable to find any studies proving that children who are trained are any more successful at warding off attackers than untrained children. Most victims have been given such warnings by loving parents, yet have fallen prey. Unfortunately, the training has brought confusion into non-abuse situations like healthy tickling and bathing, and heightened the anxiety levels of children.[1]

Some offenders are more effective in their threats or methods of intimidation or instilling guilt than others. From a child's perspective, it can seem impossible to resist or to tell what has happened. For instance, being told that your whole family will be killed if you dare to speak out, presents too great a risk to take. Imagine sitting on a beloved grandpa's knee, being told that if you say anything about him touching you in the wrong place, he will be taken to jail, and it will be your fault for telling on him.

On top of failing to prevent the actual victimization, we can unthinkingly impose guilt upon children for failing to alert anyone to what is happening. It may send the message that they are at fault for the assault.

Another problem with counting on children to identify molesters is that for a child to tell about a potential molester, he or she has to be subjected to an approach, if not an actual victimization.

My hope in writing this booklet is that children will be protected before they find themselves face to face with a molester.

This series has not been designed to make parents, or anyone

1. D. Finkelhor and J. Dziuba-Leatherman, (1995). Victimization prevention programs: A national survey of children's exposure and reactions, Child Abuse & Neglect, 19: 129-39.

caring for children, imagine a predator to be behind every bush. It's not necessary to become suspicious of everyone within one's circle of activities. The purpose is to bring *heightened awareness* in *warranted situations* and the ability to relax where there are no threats to safety.

Who am I?

Who am I? I'm a mom / grandma / former social worker/teacher who failed to recognize the signs of child sexual abuse in my own home. Following the confession of my ex-husband, my family was shattered. We lost everything we held dear as a result of his secret addiction to pornography and subsequent crimes of child sexual abuse – and as a result of my misplaced trust.

I had been trained in areas of abnormal psychology through my university years; but in one planet-stopping moment of hearing his confession, I came to the painful realization that the skills of manipulation are so finely tuned in the heart of a predator, that recognition of his plans or actions can be almost impossible to suspect by anyone who is not equipped with equal skills of detection.

My question became, "If I could have experienced a thirty-eight-year marriage and not known what was happening right in my own home, how could any young mom 'out there' be expected to recognize the warning signs of a predator and protect her children?" Hence my desire to share insights that only someone in a situation such as mine could have gained.

People wonder how I could have lived in a marriage where there was so much deception that my husband became a virtual stranger.[2] The answer is that deception hides truth and when one trusts someone,

2 See booklet #9 in the *Predator-Proof Your Family Series, The Husband I Never Knew.*

there is no sense of needing to look for signs of wrong-doing. It is only when one recognizes the signs of deception that one is stirred to search for them. Awareness means never relaxing your antenna.

I trusted someone who was not worthy of trust. One of my greatest regrets will always be trusting the perpetrator rather than immediately believing a precious victim.

Unfortunately, trust cannot be assumed. It has to be tested in the fire of insights, wisdom and warning signs. If one does not know what the warning signs are, it's impossible to rest in substantiated trust.

While the charges of child sexual abuse against my ex-husband resulted in the dismantling of our family, I shall always be grateful for the courage of my granddaughter who charged him and broke the dark secret that had kept her trapped in abuse for so many years.

The first edition of this series of booklets was written in a somewhat clinical way, not revealing our personal experience. However, when my granddaughter said, "Grandma, if you're going to tell the story, you need to tell the whole story," I determined to drop the curtain of self-protection and reveal my deeper purpose in writing.

Predators count on veils of secrecy to protect and hide them. Speaking out – breaking the deep, dark secret – is the road to freedom, healing, and justice.

I can't change the past in my own home, but perhaps the future for some other children and families can be altered.

As a handbook for predator-proofing our children, the mandate of this booklet is to point the way to best practices for protecting our kids from predators of all kinds – from pimps and traffickers to neighborhood pedophiles, to strangers who you had thought were friends or family.

For anyone who might wonder, this series has not been written within a context of revenge. Quite the contrary. Although I divorced my husband and our paths took different directions following his release from prison, I was able to forgive[3] him to the degree that I do not have to walk in bitterness – for which I am grateful.

Teaching the Importance of Being Trustworthy

When parents count on children to identify molesters, they have to rely on character qualities that may not yet be fully developed. The situation can become complicated when it involves trusting children who don't necessarily always tell the truth.

I doubt that one of us can claim to have never told a lie as a child. Those of us who have become truthful adults remember how and why we grew in integrity. It's a process of growth of values within a context that confirms the development. While immaturity can be a factor in evaluating the reality of a situation, it must never be the reason for distrusting the words of a possible victim of abuse.

What happens when kids do exactly as we've told them to do – and then we don't believe them (when they really need us to) because they've told lies in the past?

In 2006, I found myself caught between declarations of absolute innocence of my husband of thirty-eight years (whom I assumed to be trustworthy) and shocking charges of his guilt by one of my granddaughters who, at that time, had an underdeveloped commitment to truthfulness. She had struggled with truth issues as a child. Now I understand that she had been trained, through being victimized, to be deceptive.

---

[3] Forgiveness doesn't mean the offender gets freed from his/her consequences; it means the one who forgives gets freed from being bound to the pain of his/her actions.

Today, when I look back at all that happened under my radar, I weep. I was living my life devoid of reality, unaware of the dynamics and activities in my own home. Because I believed my husband and didn't believe my granddaughter when she revealed the truth, the fabric of my sweet relationship with her suffered a destructive rip that no patch of attempted forgiveness has been able to eradicate. I was the adult. She was the child. In her heart, she was no doubt crying out for me to see beneath the secret she was forced to keep. I was supposed to be able to protect her; but the responsibility for protection in our home had been shifted (in her eyes) to this precious child, upon whose shoulders rested the continuation of our whole family structure. Not only did I not protect her from my husband; I didn't believe her in her traumatic moment of revelation. She and her father, my son, had to endure five days of me trying to figure out why she would tell such a terrible lie. Burned into my memory are my son's words on the other end of my cell phone on day three, "If you don't believe us, you are dead to me."

When my husband finally confessed, after that horrendous five days of me being torn between the most important people in my life, and I asked my granddaughter to forgive me for not believing her, it was too late. I had trusted the wrong person and had not been there for her in one of the most critical times of her life. She was gracious at the time and spoke words of forgiveness, but the pain of not being believed in that crucial time still needs to be healed. I can only hope that through time, genuine understanding and forgiveness will be distilled.

It's been a long road with my precious son, but I'll never forget driving to his home that night after the confession. He was just returning from somewhere, and we arrived at the same time. It was a cold, snowy January night. He wrapped me up in his arms as we stood shivering in shock and cold. Big snowflakes drifted down through the dark, winter sky. We had both been through so much, and it wasn't over. Scarred restoration.

Little did we know that my fourteen-year-old granddaughter, not yet asleep, was watching from an upstairs window, yearning to come down and be part of the hug, but not knowing how.

Children today can find themselves in a myriad of circumstances where manipulative adults instruct them not to say this or that, particularly in situations of abuse and custody battles. When adults teach children to be deceptive, there's no wonder truth is in short supply. Any adult who lies to a child, thus teaching them to lie by example, will have much for which to answer.

Children must be taught, encouraged, coached, mentored in truth-telling. It is critical, not only so that we can believe them, but to give them the security of knowing they'll be believed if they tell what is going on in their lives – because of their history of trustworthiness.

Obviously, we have to kick it up a notch and identify people who may harm our children before they get a chance to try. Teaching them to be trustworthy provides a valuable layer of protection.

We're Living in a Different World

Child molestation is nothing new. It's been around since the dawn of time, rotting the fabric of society. For many years, it was discussed only in whispers, but more recently, newspapers have become more and more filled with stories of the sexual assault of children. The 2017 *Me Too* movement blew the lid off of painful secrets that simmered for many years.

Pedophiles used to live like solitary moles, furtively looking at obscene photos of children in the dark corners of their lives. They had no one to talk to about their interests because they were too shameful.

Suddenly, the advent of the Internet gave them a forum for discussion with like-minded predators. Where soul-destroying pictures were once so difficult to procure, millions of images of depravity are now available instantly – with the click of a mouse.

There's strength in numbers. Reinforcement brought an increased boldness. Child-molesters began trading images and videoing scenes of the sexual abuse of children; brainwashing themselves into thinking they were some kind of an oppressed minority group.

As in the case of my ex-husband, addiction to pornography is most often a precursor to child molestation. That does not mean that everyone who watches porn will molest a child or sexually assault an adult – it just means that it increases the possibility of it happening.

Michael Brière was the 36-year-old computer programmer who raped, murdered and dismembered beautiful ten-year-old Holly Jones in Toronto in 2003. Holly had been walking home from a friend's house and innocently passed Brière's house on the way. Unbeknownst to anyone, he had been looking at child pornography on the Web and had begun to have fantasies about having sex with a child. After a couple of years of indulging in his "dark secret," he had become consumed with the idea. "I really wanted to have sex with a child. And that was all-consuming. I just came out of my place, and she was just there." For the sake of forty minutes of indulging his darkest fantasy, Brière lost his place in the world and Holly was lost to the world.

It's a different world. A report released in 2018 from the Canadian Centre for Child Protection revealed that nearly 1,300 Canadian children have been victims of sexual offenses carried out — or alleged to have been carried out — by school employees in the last twenty years. The report detailed the findings from an examination of sexual assault cases involving staff at kindergarten to Grade Twelve schools in Canada. It reported that 714 employees, or former employees, were linked to sexual offenses against schoolchildren between 1997 and 2017. Officials believe the study is the most comprehensive inventory of child sexual abuse involving school employees in Canadian history. With the Canadian population being only one-tenth of that in the USA, the numbers are probably ten times as high in America.

When parents can't send Johnny or Susie off to school without worrying about school employees or the walk home, there's a problem. Things have to change. We have to find ways to keep children safe and clean up the moral air we breathe.

Child and Teen Sex Trafficking
21st- Century Slavery

To me, the scariest thing on earth would be to have a child or teen trapped in the most horrendous evil of all: sex trafficking. The lucrative commodity in this multi-billion-dollar industry is children and teens who are moved from town to town all over the world to service the perversions of men with wallets. Each victim brings in from $260,000 to $280,000 per year for traffickers in North America. There are over 40 million slaves in the world today.[4]

In his 2018 book *The True Story of Canadian Human Trafficking,* Paul H. Bogue presents a comprehensive understanding of the world of dangers faced by our families.

---

4. Bogue, Paul H. (2018) *The True Story of Canadian Human Trafficking,* Castle Quay Books, Canada

These dangers have been augmented by the changes in family structures and societal norms. Increased isolation of kids and teens with lessened parental involvement, the dynamics of technology and 21st-century culture leaves them less connected on every level.

It is a known fact that where home and family relationships and communication are prioritized, the dangers are lessened because predators look for potential victims who are vulnerable to their advances. Impressionable young girls without solid anchors can be easy to intimidate and then easy to control.

When a young girl enjoys a stable, loving relationship with her father and mother, she doesn't crave assurances of her worth or beauty. She knows she's loved and treasured. She doesn't need a pimp with a plan to tell her she's beautiful and then woo her away with lies.

On the flip side, when an insecure, lonely young girl scrolling through her phone decides to respond to a cute stranger who shows interest, she can open herself up to years of torture, terror, prostitution, and devastation – if not death. One naive meeting can seal the deal.

When a reporter asked a girl rescued from sex trafficking what one thing could have prevented her from falling prey to the pimp, she said this: "If only my father had paid more attention to me. Something happens when a daddy takes a lot of time for his little girl. It's like there's this protective net that gets built around her. Enables her to feel real love. Enables her to spot creeps. But when Daddy's not around, or if there's sexual abuse, it's like that covering disappears and we're open prey. Every girl I've talked to – every single rescued victim, to a one – they all say the same thing. If only their dads would have taken more time with them. I'm not saying the dads are always to blame. It's just what the girls I've talked to say."[5]

5. Bogue, Paul H. (2018) *The True Story of Canadian Human Trafficking,* Castle Quay Books, Canada, p.243

She went on to say, "I want girls to know two things. First, you are being targeted. I know we want to live in a fun, free world. But that's not what this world is. There are many, many traffickers and they are hunting for you at malls. At community clubs. At places of worship. And especially online. They're reading your profiles. Studying what you say. Figuring out a way into your life. Second, I want you to know that whatever you're going through, you don't need to sacrifice yourself for love. And if a guy really does love you, bring him to meet your family. Creeps hate families. But real guys will want to know your parents and friends. A real guy will respect you, honor you and build you up."[6]

Because human trafficking stories are all different, strong families are not guarantees for the safety of the children, but they are huge protective factors

Five Main Entry Points Into Trafficking

There are five main entry points into trafficking.[7] While this is a generalization, it is a practical overview geared to helping parents understand the danger and protect their kids.

1. The runaway pickup girl who has left home, thinking she can make it on her own. Any girl on the street is approached within twenty-four hours, offered the basic necessities in exchange for a few favors, and then told she has to sell her body or be killed.

2. The guerilla method. Snatch and grab. The victim is taken from a street, a park, a home – wherever. He or she is then thrown into a vehicle, beaten, drugged, conditioned and sold to man after man.

6. Bogue, Paul H. (2018) *The True Story of Canadian Human Trafficking,* Castle Quay Books, Canada, p.306
7. Ibid, p.243

3. The renegades. Girls who decide to 'dabble' in prostitution, with the lure of big money, usually decide they want the "protection" of a pimp; only to discover that their supposed bodyguards care only about the money they can make and will keep most, if not all, of it.

4. Female "friends" in the industry introduce girls to their trafficker, show her how to turn tricks, get her into drugs and start her into the downward spiral.

5. The lover-boy method – the most common entry point. A man approaches a girl wherever she is, whether in-person or online. He's fishing – contacting dozens of girls, looking for one who will bite. It doesn't matter who she is; rich, poor, upper-class, lower-class, religious, secular, black, white or purple. He doesn't care; he's just looking for someone who will believe he cares about her long enough to enable him to reel her in. He tells her how gorgeous she is, how cool. He methodically builds the relationship without connecting to her parents; giving her jewelry and all kinds of material gifts. He gradually undermines her family relationships until she gives him her heart and buys into the idea that he can make her dreams come true. Then comes the idea of a little trip out of town where he "sets the lure." Telling her they need a lot of money to be able to live the kind of life they want together, he convinces her how easy and lucrative it would be to turn a few tricks. Just a few – at first. But then more and more. If she wakes up and tries to leave, he shatters the pretense (that he no longer needs) and gets her hooked on drugs or threatens to kill her or her family. At this point, the "relationship" becomes one of total slavery. He owns her, and she is trapped in her nightmare.

How big is the problem? From coast to coast, you can't go more than a half-mile without a girl being held against her will.[8]

But we don't have to freeze in fear for our kids; we just have to kick it up a notch to protect them.

Kicking it Up a Notch

But sex trafficking is only one way a child's life can be forever changed through abuse. What about the one out of two girls or one out of three boys who are victimized by friends, family or strangers who use them only to service their own perversions?

We used to feel as though we were doing our jobs as parents by hiring a decent-looking babysitter if we were going out, locking our doors at night and generally keeping an eye on the kids at playgrounds, theme parks, and shopping malls.

It's not enough. We have to find ways to protect our children not only from strangers we've never met but from strangers who may live in our own homes or strangers who we've counted among our friends for many years.

Protecting a child from a stranger who wants to abduct a child for the purposes of a sex crime is generally a matter of logistics – doing everything we can to make sure that the child cannot be taken. But who can be with a child 24 / 7? However it's managed, diligence in making sure a child is not left vulnerable is worth every effort.

Protecting a child from a manipulative predator (who, in eighty percent of the cases is known to the child or the parents) can present complex challenges, as it involves screening every association the child experiences. In Booklet # Two, *Who is the Predator?* I

---

8. Bogue, Paul H. (2018) *The True Story of Canadian Human Trafficking*, Castle Quay Books, Canada, p.105

compiled a checklist that could help warn of possible dangers. We must go through it, considering every characteristic of every friend, acquaintance and family member who has access to our children and make informed choices about whom we allow to spend time with them. For the benefit of those who may not have Booklet # Two, I have reprinted these warning signs in Appendix A, "**Recognize the Warning Signs,**" at the back of this booklet. Because all child-molesters are finely tuned manipulators, I've also reprinted **"The Manipulative Molester"** in Appendix B. However, I suggest you read the full versions of all booklets in this series for more in-depth understanding and further insights.

At this point in the history of our society, limiting opportunities for anyone to interfere with a child is critical.

Kicking it up a notch means the following:

- Being hands-on parents, giving primary priority to children until they are old enough to look after themselves.
- Putting alarms in children's and grandchildren's bedrooms at adult height (so they're not going off with the dog).
- Keeping both eyes on kids.
- Holding their hands (or using a harness) until they are of a reasonable age (no matter how much they may protest).
- Teaching children to look for a mommy with kids or grandma if they get separated from you in a mall because female shoppers are a lot more plentiful than security guards and there is a higher probability of predators being male than female.
- Staying home with children as much as possible until they get old enough to stay alone, minimizing babysitter risks.
- Screening potential caregivers for criminal offenses through local and federal law-enforcement agencies; not being afraid to request the person's birth date, social security number and a list

of places where they have lived. Those will be needed for proper screening.

- Occasionally popping in unannounced on the babysitter.
- Being meticulously on time whenever a child is expecting to be picked up from extracurricular activities or wherever.
- Establishing who is allowed in the house with a babysitter while you're away and following-up to make sure your expectations have been met.
- Establishing rules where sleep-overs are allowed, even with relatives. Being satisfied that no teen or adult will be able to have access to your child's bed while he or she is sleeping.
- Keeping current with your child regarding any secrets anyone may be requiring him or her to keep. Teaching children that if any teen or adult asks them to keep a secret, no matter how bad it may be, they need to tell you immediately and not be afraid of consequences from the person who wanted them to keep the secret. Assuring your child that it's safe to share secrets with you.
- Reading in a lawn chair or gardening when your kids play outside – anything that puts you with them.
- Spending time at the home of your children's friends before allowing them to visit there on their own. If something feels uncomfortable, it may be a red-light warning. Don't ignore it.
- Putting the safety of your children before fears of "hurting someone's feelings" through your conscientious efforts on behalf of their safety.
- Encouraging children to bring their friends home to your house instead of going to theirs – knowing their friends.
- Planning entertainment that involves your children.
- Becoming involved in their activities. Involved parents are a big "turn off" for predators.
- Not advertising your child's name on a backpack, necklace or

other personal items.

- Reducing the desirability of your child by not dressing a little girl in alluring clothing.
- Keeping in mind the fact that predators look for ease of approach and ease of retreat.
- Making sure to choose a day-care or school with an open-door policy that allows full visibility from the hallway at all times, and making it clear that your child is not to be left with anyone but the primary caregiver without your knowledge.
- Making sure that any organization in which your child is involved (church, school, clubs) has protocols, such as Plan to Protect®, in place for the proper care of your child. Asking for an outline of their employee training.
- Attending your children's lessons and other activities, or sending someone you trust to accompany them.
- Not allowing the Internet in the privacy of a bedroom.
- Taking the cameras off of your computers. The judgment area of the brain is not fully matured until age thirty; so trusting a child in a room alone with a camera and access to chat rooms is not wise. It's not so much about trusting the child as it is about recognizing the physiological limitations on his or her safety.
- Reinstating family discussions and family meals where open communication with the child is firmly established – also one-on-one open communication.
- Initiating open-ended communication. "How was your day?" or "Did you have fun at Johnny's?" may not give a child the opening they need to tell you what's really on their hearts. Asking, "Is there anything else you'd like to talk about?" or "Is there anything worrying you," may help open the door for things that need to be discussed.
- Supplying kids with emergency cell phones or GPS gadgets. I

prefer smartwatches that send and receive texts because they are strapped onto the child's wrist and don't require data plans.

- Supplying kids with information; such as what to do if they've been locked in a car trunk. Play-rehearsing such scenarios in a non-threatening, informative, reassuring environment.
- Having up-to-date photos and fingerprints of the child in case they are ever needed. (Micro-chipping is unnecessary and creates its own issues.)
- Knowing what numbers to call in case of emergency. Having them always accessible.
- Teaching a child to self-protect with the buddy system – always having someone know the "who, what and where" answers: who are you with, what are you doing, and where are you going.
- Teaching children that if a stranger tries to take them, their voices and legs are their best defense. They need to go crazy, making it impossible for the stranger to get a grip on them; getting down on the ground, kicking, screaming, biting if a hand is put over their mouths, yelling, "Stranger, stranger, call 911." Rehearsing scenarios, so children are familiar with what to do.
- Teaching children that their bodies are their own and that it's okay to decline any touching or contact that makes them uncomfortable; particularly on parts that are usually covered by a bathing suit or underwear (with the exception of bath-time towelling by a parent or guardian, and visits to the doctor with a nurse present).
- Teaching children that if they feel uncomfortable, they need to get out of the situation; assuring them that if that means yelling, they won't get into trouble.
- Teaching children to tell about anyone who exposes themselves or shows them pictures of private parts.
- Teaching children that it's okay to talk back to an adult if they're

told to do something that doesn't seem right to them. Instructing them to call you in such a situation.

- Taking parenting courses to increase confidence in being in control of your child.
- Never ignoring a child's protests about spending time with a particular adult; encouraging the child to tell you why and what is going on there. Believing him or her.
- Facing the reality that you are taking a grave risk if you send your child off on a solitary walk or bike ride. Any parent of a child who has been taken will say they would gladly have put their own interests aside to bike or walk with the child if they had the opportunity to do things over again. We are living in a different world than the one in which we were raised, and we cannot pretend that the danger rate is the same as it used to be.
- Paying special attention to friendships involving older persons, even older teens. Never letting your guard down.
- Helping kids going through puberty to manage their own sexual feelings without veering towards pornography or premature sexual activity.
- Daring to be vocal about setting boundaries with girlfriends and boyfriends and enforcing them. Being prepared to be the most unpopular person in their world at that moment.
- Handling peer pressure regarding pornography and violent or sexual video games.
- Making your home a porn-free environment.
- Being familiar with the staff and curriculum at your child's school.
- Being pro-active in guiding your children in the development of positive values and mindful awareness of their environment.
- Watching carefully for signs of abuse – physical and emotional.
- Not being afraid to ask questions.

Many parents think they have to cave in to a child's contention of lack of trust, to communicate confidence. Acquiescing when a child accuses, "You don't trust me," needs to be met with a firm, "It's not about trusting you – it's about not trusting people who don't have your best interests at heart and about waiting for your brain to mature in the area of judgment." Educating a child about the stages of brain development can help a child to monitor himself/herself.

Besides the benefit of providing more safety for our children, this is the kind of stuff that makes for close families later on. It's hands-on caring. The other benefit is that it will make the child feel more secure.

Is it stifling? Smothering? Over-protective? Paranoid? When balanced against loss or harm, those words lose any meaning.

Whom Can We Trust?

No one should ever have to distrust the safety of a grandparent's home or the honor of a best friend around one's children; but that was the way it used to be, not the way it is today. Even after screening people, how do we know for sure who the molesters will be? Can we trust no one? Is everyone suspect? Do we have to live totally paranoid lives?

It's not about blanket distrust or paranoia. Just as we don't have to fear being labeled paranoid if we put life vests on our kids in a boat, we don't have to fear similar judgments when we eliminate situations where children could be at risk.

It's about paying closer attention and listening to gut instincts that something may not be right. It's about forcing ourselves to pursue suspicion rather than turning a blind eye to odd behavior, even in those we may love. If we don't allow our minds to consider the horror of them being potential predators, we may miss the critical indicators and put our children in peril.

Does this mean that if we have suspicions about Uncle Harold, we should deny him access to his nieces or nephews?

No. It merely means that, as parents or grandparents, we don't allow Johnny or Susie out of our sight at family reunions and we don't allow Uncle Harold to drive them home. No one has to know about our concerns. Running around like frazzled scatterbrains expressing suspicion about everyone is entirely counterproductive. It can actually work in the manipulator's advantage because it will result in more people telling you to calm down and potentially lead you to drop your guard to be more socially acceptable.

Does this mean we have to report every suspicion to the police or that we have to prove that anyone exhibiting some or all of the warning signs is a predator?

No. It should be a criminal offense to ruin a reputation without concrete evidence. We merely have to step up to the plate and take responsibility for watching our children.

In most cases where a molester begins to groom a child (and the adults around the child) to allow him to make his move if access to the child is removed, the danger will be eliminated. If your instincts sound the slightest alarm, just remove the child. Don't allow yourself to be manipulated into allowing even a moment of unsupervised access again. Then, quietly keep an eye on the person in question for the protection of other children.

The "Grooming" Process

Once a pedophile sets his sights on a particular child, a process of *grooming*, almost like *wooing* begins. It's a process of gaining trust with his victims, getting them ready for what he wants to do. Because parents or caregivers can be viewed as nuisance barriers for predators, gaining access to a child often involves the grooming of the parents as well as the child.

The process of grooming can involve a lengthy period of time, with nothing happening abruptly. The aspect of being gradual is vital. The last thing the predator wants to arouse is suspicion. Everything has to look and feel natural. It's a carefully orchestrated process of building trust, planting thoughts in people's minds, establishing precedents and conditioning victims to accept all the events and responses necessary for the actual victimization to occur as being normal.

Predators masquerading as normal people are often well-received by parents. Many seem so nice, so accommodating, so helpful. What lovely people, we think.

Many, if not most, people *are* truly wonderful. The confusion lies in separating genuinely wonderful people from manipulative predators.

While it's critical to be aware of possible bad apples, it's also critical to maintain equilibrium, recognizing that there are many fine people who truly have the child's best interests at heart.

Dr. Anna Salter, Ph.D., who has worked with and written extensively about sex offenders, notes that, "a double life is prevalent among all types of sex offenders.... The front that offenders typically offer to the outside world is usually a 'good person,' someone who the community believes has a good character and would never do such a thing."[9]

---

9. Salter, Anna C. (2003). *Predators: Pedophiles, Rapists and Other Sex Offenders* , New York: Basic Books, p.34.

Dr. Salter found that child-molesters do whatever they can to allow themselves to have access to children while concealing their activities. This usually means finding positions that allow them to be close to children. They generally act responsible socially and appear to be sincere, truthful people. Parents and others accept them at face value, believing the persona, thereby allowing the offender to have free and easy access to the child.

From material they compiled from predators, Elliott, Browne, and Kilcoyne found that child-sex offenders rarely choose their victims indiscriminately. They choose and set them up carefully. A child experiencing parental neglect is highly vulnerable. Pedophiles often pick children from broken families whose parents are distracted by their problems.

The way they operate is by seeking to exploit the emotional void in a lonely child's life by befriending them and showering them with gifts, attention and sometimes money. Bribery and games are commonly used, with the offender slowly desensitizing the child through touch, sex-talk, and persuasion.[10]

Dr. Salter recounts the careful planning a young pedophile put into grooming a victim:[11]

> "When a person like myself wants to obtain access to a child, you don't just go up and get the child and sexually molest the child. There's a process of obtaining the child's friendship and, in my case, also obtaining the family's friendship and their trust. When you get their trust, that's when the child becomes vulnerable, and you can molest the child."

10. Elliott, M., Browne, K., & Kilcoyne, J. (1995). Child Sexual Abuse Prevention: What Offenders Tell Us, Child Abuse & Neglect, 579-94.
11. Salter, Anna C. (2003). *Predators: Pedophiles, Rapists and Other Sex Offenders* , New York: Basic Books, p.42.

This is a clear demonstration of the gradual grooming process in which the predator manipulates the child into participating.

Following my ex-husband's release from prison, I contacted him and told him about the series of booklets I was writing to help parents identify predators and protect children. When I asked him if he would be willing to be interviewed, sharing his perspective to give deeper insight to parents wanting to know how to protect their kids most effectively, he did not hesitate but agreed without reservation. He was broken and open to exposing his shame if it could, in any way, dissuade anyone else from targeting a child or acting on fantasies – or if it could in any way bring healing to his victims or give insight into the pandemic of child molestation.

He arrived one cold, fall morning at my apartment. After having shared a home for thirty-eight years, it was awkward inviting him into my sanctuary. He didn't belong here, but I was grateful for his willingness to contribute to my work. I motioned him to a sofa that had once belonged to us both, and he sat down.

There wasn't a lot of small talk. I plugged in my equipment, hoping to glean insights that would help other moms to spot potential danger for their kids. The whole scenario was eerily other-worldly. How could this even be happening? How could thirty-eight years together end with a cold, metal microphone between us? How does one take the leap from a marital relationship to a clinical interview? Coming to terms with the fact that my place in his life had been more about serving as a respectable front for his inner/other life than any genuine relationship had not been easy. I had to ignore myself and focus on the reason for my work. I turned on the recorder and began. For the purposes of the interview, I've called him "Matt."

The following is a brief snippet of the interview. A fuller excerpt can be found in Booklet # Two in this series *Who is the Predator?*

> Matt: While I had begun to fantasize about schoolgirls, I never intended to actually get myself into a situation of molesting a child. The first time it happened, I was leading a children's church group and a young girl, who was a foster child of a family in the church, used to want to be around me all the time. She had been sexually active in a previous home and was very clingy with any male leader who would pay attention to her. She was mentally and emotionally weak and just wanted someone to love her. She wanted males to love her. One of the other leaders had to have a talk with her foster mother about how she was always making plays for the male leaders. I played on her needs. One day when I was at her home, she flipped her top up out of the blue and exposed her breasts to me. That's when I should have just told her to pull her shirt down and left the situation, but I didn't.

> Me: Did the foster parents not suspect anything?

> Matt: The girl's foster mother was very observant. I felt she was always on the outlook for the kids because she had had a previous situation where someone was suspected of molesting one of her grandkids, and so I never pushed anything, because that would have been a red flag to her. I could sense that she was always very protective.

> Me: Did you ever feel that she had any distrust of you?

> Matt: No. Not at all. In fact, it was precisely the opposite. I was very much in a position of trust with the kids.

I remember many visits to the home where this happened. We were good friends of the foster parents. I remember being uncomfortable about the fact that Matt seemed to enjoy being with the kids more than with the adults. I remember worrying that because he seemed more interested in spending time with the kids than visiting with the adults, they would think he didn't find them interesting. But I tried to brush my concerns aside because it wasn't something I could control. I rationalized it with the conclusion that he just enjoyed kids.

In the process of grooming, after establishing a friendship, the offender may start showing the child some pornography and telling him or her not to tell the parents. Alcohol or drugs may be introduced. If the child keeps the secret, the offender may proceed to the next step, gradually escalating this kind of behavior until the child is desensitized enough to participate in more sexually progressive activity. The more secrets a child keeps, the more they may hesitate to disclose the abuse, possibly feeling responsible and ashamed of the sexual acts in which they engaged.

The molester a child faces is not a statistic. He or she is a person; the outwardly caring teacher, the hockey coach or the seemingly kind relative who has worked hard to gain trust. The child is faced with either betraying that trust or keeping silent – a huge burden for a child or teen.

Managing the Internet

Pedophiles, pornographers, and child-molesters love the Internet. This is covered more extensively in Booklet #5 – *The Porn Factor*. In protecting our children from this potential source of abuse, parents can do a great deal to eliminate risk.

Kids need to be made aware that if they respond to requests for photos of themselves, they could make themselves both the victims and creators of child pornography, potentially running afoul of the law. With today's technology, there's no telling what could happen with a photo innocently sent for personal use, or what could be the actual motivations of the requester. It's no fun having a squad car drive up in one's driveway.

While we all want to trust our kids and have them believe that we trust them, the reality is that they are kids and immaturity leads people to do stupid things. According to the National Centre for Missing and Exploited Children, up to ten percent of the material they seize has been produced by older children taking compromising photos of themselves on their webcams or cell phone cameras. They e-mail the pictures to themselves from their phones and then post them on the Web. Whether the motivation is teens acting out or a lonely girl persuaded to take photos of herself by someone she has "met" on the Internet, the risk is the same.

There's no real need to have a camera on a child's computer. Just taking it off eliminates at least *one* area of risk. Granted, it's impossible to remove a camera from a cell phone. That's where instilling internal values within a child is crucial.

Parents who complain about the effects of the Internet on their children, yet do nothing to supervise or control their children's access, are guilty of neglect. If they complain about having no means to control the negative influences on their children, they need to go further than complaining and take every measure within their control to assure their child's safety. While merely removing the Internet from the home isn't going to solve the reason for concern, safeguards can be put in place. Parental popularity may not be big in such a home, but child safety is the higher value. Popularity will eventually come – as appreciation.

Parents who don't find ways to talk to their kids about sex and introduce it in a healthy way, have to know that porn is knocking at their door, waiting to pervert their child's understanding of sex, ensnaring them as victims in the multi-billion-dollar industry.

Managing the Internet means:

- Supervision: Keeping your computer in a common area, where the screen can be easily seen by anyone in the, room.
- Compiling a list of safe sites on your "Favorites" list, your child is allowed to visit: This can be easily done, with the help of your local librarian and other parents.
- Supervising postings: Forms should never be filled out without your consent. When you give your permission, be there to make sure the form is on a "secure" site which prevents information from being viewed by other people. Personal information about your child or family should not be posted on the Internet.
- Screening e-mail: Until the age you choose, take a look at what is sent to your child. Forbid the opening of anything from a stranger.
- Investing in parental controls software.

Being a parent these days is a balancing act. We have to give children enough freedom to explore the world but know when and how far to be vigilant.

When it comes right down to it, all the rules in the world cannot guarantee safety for our children. It's not just about the latest in screening software or blocking devices. It's about the kind of people we are and the atmosphere in which we raise children. Who we are on the inside and what we do when we're not online says a lot about what we'll do in a chat room. The kind of fiber we build in our children will largely determine their desires online.

I was watching an interview with Stephen Covey and his son recently and was fascinated by the quality of the son – his integrity and his insight into life. My thought was that if the fathers of this world would heed Stephen Covey's advice[12] and raise the kind of son he raised, we wouldn't be having the problems we're having. The root of much of the emptiness of young people today is simply the absence of involved parents. Fortunately, Mr. Covey has written numerous books on the subject that are available to anyone with a library card.

My good friend Jane and her husband Michael are exemplary 21st-century parents. They have two children, ages nine and eleven, who are watched like hawks and loved like puppies. Their house always has one or two extra kids around because Mike and Jane know that if their friends are welcome, the children will be more content at home. They are forever running here or there with them because proper supervision is their top priority. It's not easy now but will pay off in spades with healthy adulthoods.

If You Suspect...

Most people talk themselves out of their suspicions. It's hard to approach a situation with confidence if there is no proof. If you suspect something inappropriate may be happening, discuss it with someone you trust. Most importantly, talk to your child. Give him or her the security of being able to communicate openly with you.

There will be behavioral changes in children who are being abused.

Glenda spoke with me about her years of puzzlement – trying to understand her son's behavior.

"I was always puzzled about why my older son walked around

---

12. Stephen Covey has sold over 20 million books and *The 7 Habits of Highly Effective People* was named the #1 Most Influential Business Book of the 20th-Century. His most recent major book, *The 8th Habit,* has sold nearly 400,000 copies.

with slumped shoulders and seemed depressed so much of the time. When he and my other son would head out for the bus, he would walk straight ahead to the bus and not look back. My younger son would be smiling and waving and blowing kisses to me all the way out the driveway. It didn't make sense. My older son was handsome, smart, healthy and, as far as I knew, he had a great family life. I dressed him as well as I could, and he had parents and grandparents who loved him and who tried to make life really special for him. But he seemed angry with me so much of the time. I couldn't break through. Something was wrong, and I didn't know what it was. Now I understand why he was angry with me. It was because I failed to protect him; but I didn't suspect he was in any danger from his paternal grandfather."

If you have cause for suspicion, the most important thing is to talk with your child.

There may be:

- Nightmares
- A new knowledge of sex-related words
- A new fear of going somewhere he/she has been before, or seeing a person he/she knows
- Physical signs such as redness or injury in the genital or oral area
- Excessive masturbation or interest in playing games about sex
- Signs of emotional conflict within the child
- Depression
- Confusion
- Sulkiness
- Sleeping more than usual
- Poor posture
- Lack of self-esteem

- Difficulties with relationships
- Inability to concentrate
- Eating disorders
- Acting out
- Shoplifting or other delinquent behaviors
- Truancy or running away
- Use of alcohol or drugs
- A change in academic achievement
- Disconnection from the family
- Sneakiness with pornography

The most reliable way to determine whether your suspicions are valid is to have your child evaluated at a treatment center that specializes in sexual abuse cases. It may be helpful to find a therapist knowledgeable in the field to work with the child on behavior issues until the child is ready to disclose the abuse.

If you, yourself, have been abused, it may be that you lack the objectivity to discern what is happening in your child's life. Your super-sensitivity to the issue may be leading you to see abuse where there is none. Conversely, your emotions regarding the issue may be a roadblock to avoid dealing with the problem. If you're confused, it's important to seek the advice of a professional well-acquainted with the issues.

Being right about everything all the times is impossible. There may be times when you're wrong. The bottom line is that the best we can do is the best we can do to keep our children safe and to reassure them that they can come to us with anything that is bothering them.

If a child actually discloses the fact that he or she is being abused, believe it. While there are situations, usually in custody battles where a parent will coach a child to accuse a parent of abuse, the ruse is usually obvious. For a child to fake the trauma of an abuse victim, exhibiting the profound emotional reactions would be worthy of an Oscar.

Let the Law Deal With It

Without proof, denial is almost a sure thing from the suspect.

Glenda continues:

"Not until he was thirteen-years-old, did my son feel big enough to start saying no to his abuser and tell my husband and me, in another time of crisis, what he had been enduring for so many years. Only then did his demeanor throughout those years make sense.

"But now I deeply regret the way I handled it.

"It was the eighties and child sexual abuse was almost never in the news. I had no idea what to do and numbly tried to feel my way. No one I knew had ever had to face such a thing. I called the police anonymously and asked what would happen if I were to report the abuse. Before that, I had never had any dealings with police beyond a speeding ticket. The idea of involving them in my life was entirely foreign to me. When they said my son would probably be called to testify, I decided not to take that route, but to handle it myself because I wanted to protect my son from the trauma of the court process. He had already been through so much.

"Because I am a person of faith, I saw the condition of the abuser's dark heart as the real problem and thought the most effective way of changing it was through spiritual transformation. And so I arranged the restaurant meeting, naïvely thinking that maybe I could save my son the dreaded court process.

"When I arranged a meeting in a restaurant with the abuser and confronted him with my son's disclosure, he appeared utterly shocked and said, 'How could you even think such a thing?'

"I said, 'On top of everything you've done to my son and me, are you going to make him a liar, too?' With that, he looked down and admitted his guilt.

"So, after telling him that he would not be welcome in our home and could not see my sons again until he had dealt with his problem, I sent him off with some books that I thought would speak to the situation.

"What I didn't understand at the time was the manipulative nature of the child molester. I was still the trusting little mommy who believed that things could really be the way they appeared and that people would tell the truth. I am not saying the abuser's life could not have been transformed. However, a person has to *want* to change, or nothing is going to happen.

"Anyway, my son's molester appeared at our home after a couple of days and claimed to have had a spiritual epiphany. At first, it seemed that I had done the right thing. I believed him and thought all predatory inclinations had been washed away with the internal transformation.

"Unfortunately, the real changes that should have happened with a genuine epiphany didn't occur, and as soon as the crisis appeared to be over, he reverted to his normal personality. Not long after, he developed cancer and died.

"While some might say the situation was looked after by the cancer, if I had it to do again, I would definitely have involved the police. For one thing, it's the law. Child sexual abuse has to be reported. I didn't know that back then – and I knew nothing about the dynamics of predatory manipulation."

Child-molesters need to be punished. They need the chastisement of jail, the humiliation of walking in shackles to court, the embarrassment of donning the orange jumpsuit, the fear of the other inmates, the rudeness of the guards, the grief of losing their established lives, the insecurity of losing control of everything, and the time to think about what they have done to everyone whose shattered lives have touched theirs.

Victims need to feel that there has been justice for what they have suffered. While Glenda thought she was being kind to her son by protecting him from the trauma of a courtroom, what really happened was that she unintentionally denied him the opportunity to see justice done. That gave rise to deep anger and a sense of injustice within him. By the time she realized it, it was too late. It was more baggage that he had to sort through and carry. She wishes she could go back.

But she can't. The law is there for a purpose.

Community Protection

They say it takes a village to *raise* a child. In the same way, it takes a village to *protect* a child. While parents are the first line of defense, organized community response is vital as an active support.

Community efforts to protect against child abuse are being augmented by the fact that over the past twenty years, the issue of child abuse has become the single most critical liability issue facing insurance companies in North America. Consequently, very few insurance agencies will insure organizations and institutions against allegations of abuse unless they can prove they have a formal plan in place to ensure safety from child predators and that everything possible is being done to prevent such occurrences within the client's organization.

While it would be nice if organizations would put safety protocols in place (like *Plan to Protect®*) purely for the sake of protecting kids, this is not a perfect world, and a little nudge from insurance companies is appreciated.

In Remembrance of Victoria

Melodie Bissell, CEO of *Plan to Protect®*, wrote a blog in memory of a little girl who died at the hands of her guardians as the surrounding community turned a deaf ear.

"Victoria Adjo Climbié (November 2, 1991 – February 25, 2000) was abused and murdered by her guardians in London, England in 2000. The public outrage at her death led to a public inquiry which produced significant changes in child protection policies in the United Kingdom, including the formation of the *Every Child Matters* program; the introduction of the Children's Act of 2004 and the creation of the *Contact Point Project*, a government database that holds any information regarding abuse on children in the UK.

"At the time of her death, the numerous locations of lacerations on this wee girl's body were horrifying. Evidence showed that Victoria was beaten on a daily basis with a shoe, a coat hanger or a wooden cooking spoon and her abuser would strike her toes with a hammer. Victoria's blood was found on her uncle's football boots. He admitted that at times he would hit her with a bicycle chain.

"In her postmortem, it was found that Victoria had 128 separate injuries on her body. No area had been spared. Marks on her wrists and ankles indicated that her arms and legs had been tied together. It was the worst case of deliberate harm to a child the investigator had ever seen.

"*There were over 100 witnesses to Victoria's maltreatment and abuse.* This was not done in secret. The community services, hospitals, doctors, social workers, teachers, babysitters, neighbors all had seen the injuries and suspected the abuse but *waited for others to respond. The community did not join forces to protect the child.*

"Weeks before Victoria's death, she was taken to a local church on two separate occasions. The pastor was told that she was demon possessed and need prayer. Both times, he prayed over her and encouraged her to be a good girl and obey everything her aunt and uncle instructed her to do.

"This story is heartbreaking; not only because of the senseless death of Victoria but because so many community workers held vital information which, had it been shared, could have spared and changed her life.

"The account of Victoria Adjo Climbié's life continues to underscore the mission of *Plan to Protect*®. We want to put the tools and training for abuse recognition and prevention into the hands of every community group possible. We exist to bring understanding to those who work in schools, camps, churches, sports leagues, babysitting, piano teaching, tutoring, counseling and all aspects of child interaction, regarding the critical nature of awareness and preparedness to protect children and youth.

"We need to start working together on behalf of the most vulnerable in our society and support the significant efforts that are being made by some daily.

"Unfortunately, we have a long way to go before we win the race against abuse. We will, however, accomplish much more if we work together to create a protective environment in our communities and be proactive in initiating healing communities."

Plan to Protect®

Melodie, with her associates, has developed *Plan to Protect®,* a practical protection manual for children, youth and organizations. It has been used by over 7,500 groups since 1996 and is now the *recognized standard* for abuse prevention and vulnerable sector protection. Organizations that access their services and training report significantly increased confidence in their ability to serve the vulnerable sector because gaps in security are eliminated. Melodie says:

"At *Plan to Protect®,* we believe the battle can be won through creating winning environments for children and youth. Our *Plan to Protect®* program is a prevention plan aimed at the eradication of physical, sexual and emotional abuse of children and safeguarding them from neglect. We are committed to helping to prevent it in schools, churches, camps, daycares, clubs, and sports.

"Our team has many decades of experience in creating

safe environments for children. We have authored *Plan to Protect®* which is now the protection plan being used in 7,500 churches, schools, associations and daycares. It is a comprehensive 250-page protection plan with policies, plans, training outlines, case studies, and seventy-plus appendices. This manual is laid out in a format that both the board and the leaders can easily use to establish a strong abuse prevention policy and program. The manual is widely used across the nation. Additionally, we can process Criminal Record Checks to provide further evidence that the organization is doing everything within its ability to have child protection protocols in place.

"*Plan to Protect®* has recently launched online training. When an acceptable score is achieved, demonstrating comprehension of the policies, a Certificate of Completion can be issued. There is also a service to provide customized protocols.

"Our programs and tools meet the seven key initiatives to qualify for abuse coverage. These are generally acknowledged by experts as required to establish an effective formal abuse prevention plan.

1. Statement of Policy
2. Definition of Abuse
3. Screening Procedures
4. Operational Procedures
5. Premise Modifications
6. Annual and Ongoing Training
7. Abuse Response Protocols

"While our program will assist organizations and institutions in satisfying the requirements of insurance companies for abuse coverage, the primary motivation for keeping predators away from our children always has to be the safety of the children themselves."

Kenneth A. Hall, the president of Robertson Hall Insurance Inc., says this about *Plan to Protect®:*

"For many years, Robertson Hall Insurance has recommended *Plan to Protect®* to our client organizations. The updated version is even more user-friendly, practical and understandable for leaders as they seek effective ways to protect the children and youth in their care against potential harm, and protect their workers from false allegations. Plenty of great examples, training ideas and sample forms means that your organization doesn't have to reinvent the wheel when it comes to abuse prevention. Having the new edition and updated materials as a resource and template for abuse prevention policies and procedures is like the benefit of an expert without having one in your group. We applaud the efforts of Melodie Bissell and *Plan to Protect®* for making effective abuse prevention more achievable ..."

Lorna Dueck, CEO of C.C.C.I., journalist, and host of *Listen Up TV* wrote an article encouraging the use of the *Plan to Protect®*. The following is an excerpt:

"The story of *Plan to Protect®* is one in which I firmly believe. At a time when newspapers are inundated with stories of school, organization, league and church payouts to victims in the billions of dollars, there are individuals committed to creating safe environments for children. *Plan to Protect®* has become an invaluable tool.

"*Plan to Protect®* includes the guidelines and structure
to minimize the opportunities for child abuse to occur.
Organizations in Canada working with children and youth
are rising to the challenge and implementing policies and
procedures to ward off predators. I would like to believe our
children are now safe, but the stories of abuse continue to be
reported. Many a tear falls from heaven every time a child is
abused. Crime stories continue to fill our airwaves. Predators
are only a mouse click away.

"The story needs to be told of those who are screening out
the predators, and providing protection so that our children
cannot only survive but thrive. We cannot rest on our laurels;
we must continually strive to protect children one at a time...

"You may be one of those defenders protecting our children in
schools, camps, daycares, churches, and clubs. I encourage you
not to let your efforts fall flat; do not let down your guard. You
have a part to play in this plan to protect our kids!

"Hats off to the authors of *Plan to Protect®* and its founders,
who give us the tools to cherish and protect the most valuable
asset we have – our children!"

Conclusion

Our society needs a paradigm shift. We have to change our mindset
regarding the protection of our kids. We're living in a different world
than the one in which we grew up.

Never have the purveyors of pornography had such a widespread
influence on the development of our boys and girls and been so
available to everyone, right in their own homes.

Never before have pedophiles, and child-molesters had a peer group of like-minded individuals with whom they can connect any hour of the day or night, empowering and seemingly legitimizing each other through their numbers.

Never have our prisons been so crowded with sex-offenders, most of whom will one day be set free – some rehabilitated, others not.

Our kids need the preparation, protection and prevention protocols required by today's world to be in place for them. However, no matter how many community protection systems are put in place, the front-line battle has to start before kids get to the front doors of our homes.

The paradigm shift has to happen on several levels.

- Individually: Where individual values have fallen prey to apathy or dark influences, each of us needs to have our minds renewed to a wholesome thought-life. We need to value things like kindness, integrity, mentoring, patience, consideration, concern for others, gratitude, generosity, forgiveness, restorative justice, and wisdom.
- In families: Only the members of a family see what happens behind closed doors. Families need to be vigilant and fiercely protect their most vulnerable members. They must dare to inquire when suspicions arise.
- In institutions: Institutions and organizations must go beyond caring about insurance issues in their approach to the people they serve or employ. Protection of those within their sphere of influence must be a priority regarding caring about their individual safety.
- In judicial courts: Preventive deterrents to child sexual abuse need to be examined and increased to ensure the strongest

obstacles possible to indulgence in harming children and teens. We applaud modern-day heroes like Joy Smith, a Canadian Member of Parliament, who struggled and prevailed in her efforts to build support for a human trafficking bill. Thanks to her and her team, minimum sentences of five years are ensured for anyone convicted of luring young people into sex slavery. In the USA, Jillian Gilchrest, who leads the Trafficking in Persons Council, developed legislation to increase the penalty for the crime of trafficking in persons to a Class A felony, punishable by up to twenty-five years in prison. Criminal law is a way to establish societal norms.

- In software development and manufacturing: Internet companies like Google and Microsoft have been working with law enforcement for years to stop pedophiles from sharing illegal pictures on the web. They actively remove child sexual abuse imagery when it is found and immediately report abuse to the authorities. But there's always more that can be done. They should be key influencers in encouraging the engineering of games that are healthy for young minds. They need to be leaders in positive trends rather than responders to negative societal trends.

- In education: In 2014, a radical sex-ed curriculum, which outraged parents, was introduced in Ontario, Canada. The teaching of "enthusiastic sexual consent" was to be weaved throughout it, beginning in Grade One, with no mention of love or marriage. It was to become progressively more explicit in each grade. Thankfully, with the 2018 change in government, the controversial curriculum is being removed, but it was a wake-up call to recognize the social engineering which can change a society's approach to healthy sexuality. Protecting our kids from child sexual abuse involves being aware of what they are being taught anywhere that people have the power and access to speak into their lives. Parents need to be recognized as the first educators in their children's understanding of sexuality (assuming that the parents have healthy values and are willing to be positive role models).[13] The premature sexualization that can damage the brains of children does not extend only to physical sexualization: premature mental sexualization through education is equally damaging.

In the process of renewal, we need to be highly conscious of those who do not espouse the same values and be well-educated as to their tactics.

The pendulum of our culture has swung far enough to the dark side, where we have experienced its results in the sex abuse of our children, the shattering of marriages, the disintegration of our families, the objectifying of our women, the disappearance of our men and women of integrity and the suicides of our despondent youth.

Only with a new swing of the pendulum to the light will we be able to give our children back their safe streets on which to play in the warm summer evenings. Only then will we be able to predator-proof our families with confidence.

The past is irreparable – but the future is available.

It's time to create a new, different paradigm; a new, different world.

---

13. Parents As First Educators (PAFE) supports the authority of parents over the education of their children through grassroots activis. http://www.pafe.ca

Appendix A

Recognize the Warning Signs of a Predator

Dr. Charles Whitfield found that the most effective cover a child molester has is the *desire* of people not to know. When offenders deny their guilt, people want so much to believe that it didn't happen that it resonates with their own personal hopes and beliefs about the incident.

Manipulative molesters play on the doubts of normal people that someone who appears respectable would ever do such a horrible thing. Because people don't want to believe it, if someone they care about is charged with a sexual crime, they try desperately to find some other logical explanation for the child's disclosure. Because the majority of people are not suspicious and generally trust others, particularly if they are attractive and polite, they enable child-molesters to harm children.

In the course of researching her book, *Identifying Child-molesters*,[14] Dr. Carla van Dam interviewed over 300 molesters who exhibited similar types of behaviors in social situations. While there is no precise profile to identify predators, these common behaviors provide us with a general pattern to watch for. If an individual shows enough of these behaviors to arouse concern, he needs to be considered too risky to allow unsupervised around our children.

No predator will exhibit all of the signs common to molesters, simply because of human individuality. However, he or she will generally exhibit a combination of the items in the following list:

---

14. Van Dam, Carla (2001). *Identifying Child-molesters, Preventing Child Sexual Abuse by Recognizing the Patterns of the Offenders,* New York: The Halworth Maltreatment and Trauma Press.

- Projecting a general feeling of discomfort onto the people in his or her presence
- Paying particular attention to a needy child.
- Showing a preference for association with children.
- Maintenance of few friendships in his/her own age bracket.
- Having structured access to children. To groom a child and his or her parents for the abuse, a child molester has to have a legitimate connection to the child that will allow for the process of time the "grooming" takes. Teaching, bus driving, sports coaching, camp counseling and volunteering to help with children's activities, all offer opportunities to be alone with children with no parental supervision.
- Encouraging a child to develop feelings, entrapping the young victim in a situation where the child feels that the abuse is legitimized by his or her feelings for the abuser. This is a psychological condition known as the "Stockholm Syndrome" where victims develop feelings of attachment to their captors. As the victims mature, the affection for the abuser usually dwindles, and the painful truth emerges.
- Having frequent changes of residence or jobs without much discussion about the reasons for the changes.
- Staying in a dysfunctional marriage. While pedophiles most often have failed marriages because of their sexual preference, they usually try to stay in the marriage to mask their true intentions. The mate becomes a "front" for a respectable life. While they may indicate to the wife that they simply have no interest in sex, the reality may be quite the opposite.
- Continuation of inappropriate association with children despite concerns expressed by others.
- Appearing to be disconnected from normal peers.
- Making reference to children in particularly exalted terms, such

as "beautiful," "adorable," or other labels that are said in a way that seems excessive.

- Appearing to have disrespect for social boundaries.
- Exhibiting behavior that seems too good to be true; perhaps being overly helpful.
- Having a desire for hobbies that seem more appropriate for a child than for an adult; like collecting toys or whatever.
- Having either a particularly charming personality or obvious 'loner' qualities; sometimes a combination of both. The charmers are socially appealing, but often lack substance in their relationships. There's no sense of genuine bonding at a heart level.
- Lacking the capacity for intimacy, resulting in emotional loneliness.
- Interacting with young teens at a peer level; engaging in conversations about sex, crushes or whatever would not normally be of interest for an adult to discuss with a teen.
- Playing with children at a peer level; tickling, play fighting, etc. to gain confidence and rapport and to make the child feel comfortable with being touched. As the child becomes desensitized to touch in appropriate places, the touch progresses to breasts and genitals.
- Responding to concerns with denial and aggression, making the concerned individual feel like a fool.
- Maintaining an image of social acceptability; often taking leadership in children's groups through which to gain the trust of parents and children alike.

Any of these warning signs need to be viewed within the context of an individual's life. For instance, if someone enjoys playing with children *in the company of other adults*, that's normal. If someone is a particularly helpful person but *doesn't seek out the company of children*, that's a wonderful thing. However, if combinations of the above qualities are evident, there's cause for concern and children need to be carefully watched around these people.

The alarming revelations of hundreds of men in the 1990's and 2000's of childhood sexual molestation by priests are a sad testimony to the compulsions of some predators who live their whole lives victimizing children until the day they are caught. Some have a history of using hundreds of children over their lifetimes. Such revelations have been shattering, but in Booklet #4 – *Predators in Pews and Pulpits,* it will become evident that one denomination is no purer than any other with regard to abuse.

Appendix B

The Manipulative Molester

One characteristic shared by all child-molesters is that they are finely tuned manipulators, and they recognize their adeptness at manipulating people to achieve their own ends.

In her book, *The Manipulative Man*, Dorothy McCoy referred to the ICD-10 (the mental health manual used in Europe) in listing the following characteristics[15] to watch for in classifying someone as a manipulator:

- A callous unconcern for the feelings of others.
- Gross and persistent attitude of irresponsibility and disregard for social norms, rules, and obligations.
- Incapacity to maintain enduring relationships, though having no difficulty in establishing them.
- Very low tolerance to frustration and a low threshold for discharge of aggression, including violence.
- Incapacity to experience guilt or to profit from experience, particularly punishment.
- Marked proneness to blame others, or to offer plausible rationalizations, for the behavior that has brought the patient into conflict with society.

While these are guidelines for identification, not every manipulator will exhibit all of the characteristics; and those who do will do so in greater and lesser degrees.

---

15. McCoy, D. (2006). *The Manipulative Man*, Adams Media, Avon, Mass. p.9.

Manipulative men hide in plain sight. They hide their true selves from everyone. If a wife tries to connect with a manipulative husband on a deep heart level, he may shrug his shoulders and say something like, "I'm not a very deep guy. This is all there is."

Although most manipulators are aware of rules and taboos, they have no respect for them. The fact that they are so crafty in hiding their deeds demonstrates that they know very well that what they are doing is wrong.

For Further Reading...

Abel, G., Becker, J., Mittleman, M., Rouleau, J., and Murphy, W. (1987). Journal of Interpersonal Violence, 2(1), March

Beauregard, M. and O'Leary, D. (2007). *The Spiritual Brain*, A Neuroscientist's Case for the Existence of the Soul, HarperOne, San Francisco, CA

Birchall, E. (1989). The Frequency of Child Abuse – What do We Really Know?, in Colton, Matthew and Vanstone, Maurice (1996). *Betrayal of Trust*; Sexual Abuse by Men Who Work With Children, , London ON: Free Association Books Ltd.

Bremner, Dr. J. Douglas (2007). The Lasting Effects of Psychological Trauma on Memory and the Hippocampus, Law and Psychiatry,

Briggs, F., & Hawkins, R.M.F. (1996). A comparison of the childhood experiences of convicted male child-molesters and men who were sexually abused in childhood and claimed to be non offenders. Child Abuse and Neglect

Browne, A., & Finkelhor, D. (1986). Initial and long-term effects: A review of the research. In D. Finkelhor, A Sourcebook on Child Sexual Abuse, Beverly Hills: Sage

Bushman, B.J., Baumeister, R.F., & Stack, A.D. (1999). Catharsis, aggression and persuasive influence: Self-fulfilling or self-defeating prophecies? Journal of Personality and Social Psychology

Butler, Sandra (1985). *Conspiracy of Silence: The Trauma of Incest,* San Francisco, Volcano Press.

Carnes, Patrick (1994). *Out of the Shadows*; Understanding Sexual Addiction, Center City, Minnesota: Hazelden Foundation

Carter, Wm. Lee (2002). *A Teen's Guide to Overcoming Sexual Abuse;* It Happened to Me, Oakland, Ca., New Harbinger Publications, Inc.

Colton, Matthew and Vanstone, Maurice (1996). *Betrayal of Trust*; Sexual Abuse by Men Who Work With Children, , London ON: Free Association Books Ltd.

Diagnostic and Statistical Manual of Mental Disorders (DSM 111-R), The American Psychological Association, 1987

Elliott, M., Browne, K., & Kilcoyne, J. (1995). *Child Sexual Abuse Prevention: What Offenders Tell Us*, Child Abuse & Neglect

Fink, Paul (2005). *Science,* Vol. 309, August.

Finkelhor, D. (1984). *Child Sexual Abuse: New Theory and Research*, New York: Free Press

Finkelhor, D. and associates (eds) (1986), *A Sourcebook on Child Sexual Abuse*, Newbury Park, CA.: Sage

Finkelhor, D., Hotaling, G., Lewis, I. and Smith, C. (1990) Sexual Abuse in a National Survey of Adult Men and Women; Prevalence Characteristics and Risk Factors, *Child Abuse and Neglect*

Finkelhor, D. (1994). The International epidemiology of child sexual abuse. Child Abuse & Neglect, 18

Finkelhor, D. and Dziuba-Leatherman, J. (1995). Victimization prevention programs: A national survey of children's exposure and reactions, Child Abuse & Neglect

Finney, Lynne D. (1992). *Reach for the Rainbow*; Advance Healing for Survivors of Sexual Abuse, New York: The Putnam Publishing Group

Forward, Susan, and Craig Buck (1979). *Betrayal of Innocence: Incest and its Devastation,* New York: Penguin Books

Genesee Justice Family (2005). *Genesee Justice 2005*; Instruments of Law, Order and Peace, Batavia, N.Y., Genesee Justice Family Research & Development

Groth, N., Burgess, A., Birnbaum, H. and Gary, T. (1978). A study of the child molester. Myths and realities. *LAE Journal of the American Criminal Justice Association*, 41(1), Winter / Spring.

Halliday, L. (1985). *Sexual Abuse:* Counseling issues and concerns. Campbell River, B.C., Ptarmigan Press

Hergenhahn, B.R. (1992). *An Introduction to the History of Psychology.* Belmont, CA:Wadsworth Publishing Company.

Hopper, Dr. J. (2007). Child Abuse: Statistics, Research and Resources Jacob Wetterling Foundation website's frequently asked questions section

Knopp, Fay Honey (1982). *Remedial Intervention in Adolescent Sex Offenses*; Nine Program Descriptions, Brooklyn, N.Y.: Faculty Press, Inc.

Leaf , Dr. Caroline (2007). *Who Switched Off My Brain?*, Switch on Your Brain, Rivonia, South Africa

Lilienfeld, Scott O. and Lambert, Kelly (Oct. 2007). Brain Stains, Scientific American

MacAulay, The Honourable Lawrence - Solicitor General Canada (2001). *High-Risk Offenders;* A Handbook for Criminal Justice Professionals, The Gov't of Canada

Marshall, Dr. W.L. and Barrett, Sylvia (1990). *Criminal Neglect;* Why Sex Offenders Go Free, Toronto: Doubleday Canada Limited

Matthews, Dr. Frederick (1995). *Breaking Silence - Creating Hope;* Help for Adults Who Molest Children, Ottawa: National Clearinghouse on Family Violence, Health Canada

McCoy, D. (2006). *The Manipulative Man,* Adams Media, Avon, Mass

Mercy, J. A. (1999). Having New Eyes: Viewing Child Sexual Abuse as a Public Health Problem. Sexual Abuse: A Journal of Research and Treatment

Michel, Lou and Herbeck, Dan, *Confessions of a Child Porn Addict,* The Buffalo News, Oct. 21, 2007

Minnery, Tom (1986). *Pornography; A Human Tragedy,* Wheaton, Illinois, Tyndale House Publishers Inc., Dr. J. Dobson

Murr, Doris C. (2004). *Dorie's Secret,* Kitchener, Ontario, Pandora Press

Peck, M. Scott (1983). *People of the Lie*, New York, Touchstone - Simon & Schuster Inc.

Posten, Carol and Lison, Karen (1990). *Reclaiming our Lives;* Hope for Adult Survivors of Incest, Boston, MA: Little, Brown & Company

Pryor, Douglas W. (1996). *Unspeakable Acts;* Why Men Sexually Abuse Children, New York and London: New York University Press

Public Health Agency of Canada (2007), National Clearinghouse on Family Violence.

Reavill, Gil (2005). *Smut;* A Sex Industry Insider (and Concerned father) says Enough is Enough, London, England, Penguin Books, Ltd.

Rush, F. (1980). *The Best Kept Secret:* Sexual abuse of children. New York, McGraw-Hill Book Company

The San Francisco Chronicle (April 3, 2005)

Salter, Anna C. (1988). *Treating Child-sex offenders and Victims;* A Practical Guide, Newbury Park, California: SAGE Publications, Inc.

Salter, Anna C. (2003). *Predators: Pedophiles, Rapists and Other Sex Offenders,* New York: Basic Books

Science Daily, July 30, 2007. News release issued by Stanford University

Medical Centre

Seligman, M.E.P. (1994). *What You Can Change and What You Can't,* New York: Alfred A. Knopf.

Sher, Julian (2007). *One Child at a Time,* Random House Canada

Singer, P. (1991). Ethics. *The New Encyclopedia Britannica*, Volume 18, Edition 15

The Holy Bible, The New International Version, Zondervan Bible Publishers, Grand Rapids, Michigan.

UN Secretary General's Study on Violence Against Children (2006) Section II.B

Van Dam, Carla (2001). *Identifying Child-molesters;* Preventing Child Sexual Abuse by Recognizing the Patterns of the Offenders, New York: The Halworth Maltreatment and Trauma Press

Wholey, Sam (1992). *When the Worst That Can Happen Already Has*; Conquering Life's Most Difficult Times, New York: Hyperion

Yantzi, Mark (1998). *Sexual Offending and Restoration*, Waterloo, Ontario and Scottdale, Pa., Herald Press

About Diane Roblin-Lee (Sharp)

Diane Roblin-Lee, award-winning author, former social-worker and educator, has (out of personal heartbreak) done extensive research in the field of child sexual abuse and the role played by pornography.

Having written over twenty books on a variety of subjects, Diane's passion has always been for the family – not only her own, but also in recognition of its importance as the basic unit of society. With the theme of family running through all of her work, Diane has been politically active, hosted several TV programs (including NiteLite for seven years) and served for many years on the board of the Heart to Heart Marriage and Family Institute.

Her legacy journal, *To My Family...My Life Legacy,* is a priceless resource for those wishing to pass on the insights, wisdom and experience gained through their lifetimes.

Remarried in 2013, Diane and her husband, Morgan Sharp, are committed to helping ensure the protection of children everywhere, through whatever means possible.

For further information on...

Training workshops and speakers
information and training materials, please contact:

Plan to Protect ®
117 Ringwood Dr., Unit #11
Stouffville, ON CAN L4A 8C1
www.plantoprotect.com 1-877-455-3555

*Other Books by Diane Roblin-Lee can be seen at
www.bydesignmedia.ca*